STURGIS

THE PHOTOGRAPHY OF MICHAEL LICHTER

MOTORBOOKS
INTERNATIONAL

Dedication

To my Irish bride of twenty years, Catherine, and my children,
Kiera and Sean, who have tolerated my quirky behavior, ideas, travels,
and late-night schedule all these years.
I love you.

———————————————

On the front cover:
2 Wheelin', Interstate-90 Wyoming, 1995

On the back cover:
That's Why We're Here, Sundance, Wyoming, 2002

On the frontispiece:
The Journey, Custer State Park, South Dakota, 2000
A number of years ago, Harley-Davidson ran a wonderful campaign with the headline,
"It's the journey, not the destination." Each day that I am on my bike, the phrase comes
to my mind like a mantra. You become part of the environment rather than moving through it
in a protective, four-wheeled shell. There is no sound insulation or climate control separating
you from out there. You become one with the stifling heat and one with the freezing cold.
You become the road. The destination drifts away.

On the title pages:
Knucklehead Couple, 1988

Contents

BY WAY OF FISHKILL

PETER FONDA

Peter Fonda,
Sturgis, South Dakota,
1998

On my way to Fishkill, New York, in 1960, I found myself in need of some good wrenching on my '57 Ford Tudor. I was going to my second season of summer stock theater and had stopped in Columbus, Ohio, to fix a steering problem with my "salesmen's–special" Ford. Having put together and taken apart my Visible V-8 many times, I had the sense to look for a good wrench rather than go to the money vacuum known as the Ford dealer.

I was in the mechanic's pit when I first heard it, a sound like no other vehicle. As I climbed out of the pit I saw a motorcycle. A big one. Its rumbling engine had a special "burble" like no other motorcycle I had heard. Its rider was dressed in greasy black jeans and several layers of topside. His head was covered by an old leather flying helmet; his eyes were hidden behind goggles from the same period. His face was masked like a highwayman, and bug specks covered all of his gear.

He peeled off the various layers of topside, throwing his big leather jacket over a cement post. He found a hose and rinsed the jacket with an old rag, the bugs coming off quite easily. The same procedure made the leather helmet and old pilot's goggles look almost brand new. As an answer to my "wow," he said that the only way to travel long distances in good leathers was to slather them with bear grease. The grime washed off his long boots in the same manner.

Because my hands were layered with grease, the rider asked for some help, thinking, I suppose, that I was a wrench. The owner of the machine shop stepped out of his little office and gave the rider a big hug.

"Got yourself a new mechanic?"

"Nope, just some college kid on his way east."

I was labeled and filed as an outsider to these men who seemed to know each other. The owner stepped into his office and came back with some cold beers, throwing one to the rider.

"You old enough?" The owner asked me.

"No sir."

"Good!" And he threw me a can.

"You ought to sell that cage, buy a motorsickle, and ride west with me to Sturgis, kid," the rider joked.

Switchback,
Iron Mountain Road,
Black Hills,
South Dakota, 1996

Some roads just need to be ridden.
Iron Mountain Road, and this
serpentine section in particular,
is one of those roads. Complete
360-degree turns raise you in
elevation, tunnels cut through rock,
pull-offs have spectacular vistas.
The time of day doesn't even matter.
Early in the morning, you get the
crisp feeling of mountain air with
the fresh smell of pine. By mid-day,
you squint as the Dakota sun glares
off the road while beating down on
your skin. By the end of the day,
the air cools and there is magic.

I was on my way to do stage work, a larger plan for life in mind, but the way the rider said "Sturgis" and the whole aura surrounding him made me think he had said "Valhalla."

"What's so fucking great about Sturgis?" I asked.

"About seventy or eighty thousand more of those." He pointed to his machine. "And an equal amount of road tales to share," he said, amiably. "You're too late for Laconia." Another Valhalla-sounding place.

"What's Laconia?"

"The oldest motorsickle rally in the U.S."

"And Sturgis?" I asked.

"The *best* motorsickle rally in the U.S."

The rider referred to his 1959 Panhead Harley-Davidson as "The Beast." Little did I know that I would make my mark in the world on a Panhead Harley-Davidson nine years later. The rider reeked of bear grease, oil, and gas, but it was kind of cool, a different kind of men's cologne. In fact, a *man's* cologne. The two men went inside, gesturing for me to follow. The walls of the room were covered with snapshots, photos of men and their machines looking tough and wise. They explained some of the photos to me, but I think they were just using me to conjure up memories for their own pleasure. They did give me another cold beer, though, so I listened with great interest. Somehow I wanted to know more about this gypsy rider. I had read Kerouac's *On the Road,* and the rider had some of that mythical dangerous magic surrounding him.

I finally made my pilgrimage to that Valhalla in 1990, for the Fiftieth Anniversary of the classic motorcycle rally of our times. But in 1990, there were 500,000 motorcycles, maybe more. And it was awesome. I rode up and down Main Street, rows of bikes lining each side of the road and a row two-deep running through its middle. Truly awesome. At least three concerts were going on at the same time for a full week. There were races, hillclimbs, and well-endowed women pulling their tops up and showing their beautiful breasts to anyone who asked. And cookouts at fields full of tents from Sturgis to Rapid City. Someone was always ready to help a fellow rider with whatever problem he or she had. It was a circus of delight for an enthusiast, and I was certainly, at the least, an enthusiast.

I have gone there nearly every summer since. I have slept on one of Mamma Pearl's couches (a very special honor for a Sturgis pilgrim). I was inducted into the Motorcycle Hall of Fame in 2000—thirty years too late, by my reckoning, but an honor as big as they come in this special world. In 1999 and Y2K, I took 52 or more friends and fellow Ugly Brothers there from my ranch in Southwestern Montana.

Over the years, I've watched the times change the Classic, and the Classic change the image of the biker I first met in Ohio so many years ago. I refuse to ride Interstates except for must-do's, and I am always in the middle of breathtaking vistas and mountain passes that rise above the tree line. Crossing out of Montana into Wyoming and back into Montana at 11,000 feet. Snowball fights in August. Spreading the ashes of fallen brothers to the winds. Valhalla.

I'll be there this year, barring an enormous amount of money in the bank and film running in the camera, and I expect to see one million riders. It's Harley-Davidson's 100th Anniversary. Hell, I'll have to ride to Milwaukee. Be a fool if I didn't.

Sturgis at Night, 1998

Some people come to bike week in the Black Hills for ten days, others for only two. Some are there
to race flat track or hill climb, others to tour the hills, but many have nothing more on their checklist
than the word *party*. No matter who comes or why, everyone visits Main Street. It may be the hub
of a usually quiet town of 7,000 people, but during Bike Week, it's ground zero, motorcycle mecca,
the epicenter around which all other activities revolve.

MIKE LICHTER COMES HOME TO STURGIS

DAVE NICHOLS, EDITOR-IN-CHIEF, EASYRIDERS MAGAZINE

Let me tell you a secret: The man who took all the stunning photographs in this book will do absolutely anything to capture the magic of the motorcycle mecca known as Sturgis. Michael Lichter has photographed custom motorcycles, bike rallies, and events for *Easyriders* magazine for over 20 years. You have to understand that Michael doesn't have to accept the hellacious assignments we send him. He actually enjoys hanging off the back of a pickup truck that is roaring down the road, dodging road kill as he shoots a squadron of chopped Harley-Davidsons and their roguish riders, his squinting face mere inches from the blur of asphalt. Mike likes shooting scenic riding scenes in the South Dakota hills at sunset and finding himself suddenly surrounded by over 200 angry buffalo.

Why does Michael enjoy shooting Sturgis so much? Well, for bikers all over the world the Sturgis Rally and Races is a homecoming. It is the one week of the year that makes the other 51 weeks of toiling and struggling worthwhile. You see, while Michael is an ace photographer, he is also a biker. When he first began shooting the Black Hills Classic (as the Sturgis Rally was once called), Mike used to throw his camera gear in a bag with a few T-shirts and bungie the pack to his Harley FL. Then he would ride to the event, shoot the hell out of it, camp out on the ground with the rest of the scooter people and then ride his leaking Shovelhead all the way home. These days Mike has a big truck to shoot from, an expert assistant named Steve Temple, a hotel room, a cell phone, a laptop computer, and far too much money invested in digital camera gear.

Like Mike, the Sturgis Rally has changed. The little race weekend and party for Pappy Hoel and his Jackpine Gypsies that began over 60 years ago has turned into the multinational corporation I like to call Biker World. Sturgis, like many large bike rallies, has gone upscale and mainstream. You'll find over 600,000 modern day motorcyclists (who just might be your doctors or lawyers in leathers) trying to experience the essence of bikerdom by making the trek home to the Black Hills. Yet, the Rally manages to keep its small-town flavor thanks to the amazing people of South Dakota and the state's rich wild-west history.

No one in the world can capture the true feeling of Sturgis better than Michael Lichter. When you look at one of Mike's shots of a group of bikes soaring through the hills with the last

Michael Lichter, On the Shovel, Wyoming, 1992

rays of sun glinting off their chrome, contrasting wildly with a purple Black Hills storm in the background, you can practically smell the ether and hear the thunder. It's because Michael lived that moment and somehow magically transferred it to film. And as I mentioned, Mike will go to any length to capture those special moments in time.

The following is a true story that expresses how far Mike will go to get a photo:

A few years ago Michael took off on his Harley FLH with Steve on the back to take some shots out in the boonies. Just as "golden hour" approached and the time was just right for those perfect scenic shots, a bee flew into the bike's path and stung Steve. Steve is extremely allergic to bee stings and proceeded to swell up like a balloon. Mike was faced with a dilemma: rush Steve to the hospital, or get a few more shots off in that perfect light. Now, I'm not saying that Steve came close to death or anything, but let's just say that Michael got the shot. When they finally headed back towards Sturgis to take care of Steve, the photographers found themselves riding with a pack of bikes. Suddenly, the bikes in front of Michael all slammed on their brakes. Long story short, Mike's bike went down and so did Mike and Steve.

Cut to the *Easyriders* crew at our hotel in Sturgis that evening enjoying a few adult beverages and watching the endless parade of motorcycles roaring by. Mike and Steve appear on the wheezing, very banged-up Harley. They are covered in cuts and scrapes (known as "road rash"), and are bleeding from numerous places. Mike dropped off Steve, who went directly to bed—apparently the adrenaline knocked the bee's poisonous present right out of his system—and then Mike got right back on the smashed bike and took off to get photos of the Sturgis nightlife downtown. This is a photographer who will not be denied!

Here's something else you should know. Michael plays the pennywhistle and over the last five or six years I've heard him play happy Irish jigs under freeway overpasses during sudden Wyoming downpours, on the beach at Daytona while waiting for bikes to appear, in seafood restaurants at Laconia while waiting for the food to come—anywhere. In other words, these photos are awash in music. While you're looking deeply at the following Sturgis gallery of photos, think of Mike and his pennywhistle and maybe, just maybe, you'll hear the light, dancing tones of Michael's special magic.

Welcome to Sturgis.

**Feeling Good,
Milwaukee to
Sturgis, 1986**

What a feeling to be riding
from Milwaukee to Sturgis
on a brand new Harley-Davidson
Softail, especially when the bike
and entire trip was from
a winning sweepstakes ticket.
Willie G. signed the gas tank
and handed over the keys.
Life should always feel so good.

Mainstreet Backlit,
Sturgis, South Dakota,
1991

Sturgis Timeline

1938 J.C. "Pappy" Hoel hosts a half-mile dirt track race for nine riders. The event, later named the Black Hills Motorcycle Classic, leads to the formation of the Jackpine Gypsies Motorcycle Club.

1942 The rally has grown to 5,000 but takes a break for World War II.

1945 The rally resumes and continues to grow.

1947 More than 400 riders participate in an AMA/Jackpine Gypsies-sponsored tour.

1954 Sturgis hosts its first dirt track races.

1961 The rally's popularity increases, and thousands make Sturgis a summer vacation.

1963 The short track at the Jackpine Gypsies club grounds is christened.

1965 The Jackpine Gypsy Tour is expanded to two days with a sleepover in Custer.

1972 CBS broadcasts a report on the rally.

1978 *Easyriders* magazine starts coverage of the rally.

1979 Michael Lichter photographs the rally for the first time.

1981 The rally attracts close to 30,000 bikers.

1985 South Dakota Governor Bill Janklow declares the rally's 45th anniversary "Pappy Hoel Week."

1990 The rally celebrates its 50th anniversary, setting a record attendance with over 350,000 riders.

1991 Sturgis Rally & Races, Inc. is formed to promote and organize the rally.

1992 The official name of the rally is changed to "The Sturgis Rally & Races."

1995 The rally has grown to take in Spearfish and Deadwood.

2000 The rally's 60th anniversary attracts the largest crowd ever, over 600,000 riders!

STURGIS

Mile markers fly by. Pavement blurs beneath my feet. A tune plays in my head to the rhythmic thumping of rubber hitting expansion cracks along the highway. My teeth keep the beat. The big twin drones as the sun beats on the left side of my face. I am heading north, as I do every August. Like an old crystal radio being fine-tuned, my mind and body become one with my bike and the world around me. I feel free. Familiar sights, warm memories waiting out a thunderstorm at the Twin Sisters truck stop; playing pool late into the night at a bar in Lusk; waiting for the sun to rise and the station to open while I sleep beside a gas pump; a locomotive's piercing headlight beam, its coal hoppers snaking behind it into the darkness. The route is one I have ridden many times before, yet each trip is unique. Another journey to Sturgis, but no two journeys to Sturgis are ever the same. Sturgis is changing. I am changing. The world is changing.

Anyone who has ridden to Sturgis is acutely aware of the area's incredible history and significance. There is something special about it that you can sense in every pore. It gives meaning to the word *freedom.* The native Sioux saw the Black Hills as a wealth of spirit and consequently respected them as sacred. The early white settlers saw them as a source of material riches, lusting after gold that had been hidden for millennia. Signs of the region's early history are all about you as you ride through and around the hills. Black Hills gold is everywhere; monuments to Native Americans abound; winding roads follow ancient trails. Of course there are the giant "faces," and the towns have curious names like Lead, Cheyenne Crossing, Silver City, and Custer. Since Sturgis, the town, and Sturgis, the rally, wouldn't exist had it not been for the Native Americans' presence and the discovery of gold in the nearby Black Hills, understanding the region's history, both written and in lore, may help the visitor to appreciate Sturgis, the experience.

Moto Madonna,
South Dakota, 1986

Gold in the Hills

Native Americans long recognized the value of the 4,500-square-mile "island in a sea of grass" they called "Paha Sapa," Lakota words that mean "hills that are black." The area was abundant with life—animals and vegetation thrived. Everything needed to sustain them was available. It was the center of their world, or the "heart of everything that is" and was treasured as such.

Before outsiders came searching for precious metals, these Native Americans had a long and rich history, albeit not written. Acknowledging this, General William T. Sherman, representing the U.S. government, and Chief Red Cloud of the Oglala Sioux signed the Fort Laramie Treaty in 1868 to ensure that the Native American way of life could continue as they knew it, uninterrupted. The following year, the treaty was ratified by the U.S. Senate and signed into law by President Andrew Johnson. According to the treaty, other than Indians, only U.S. government agents and the military were allowed into the area. Guaranteeing government protection of the Black Hills as a homeland for the Sioux, the treaty expressly prohibited trespassing by anyone else under penalty of removal and arrest.

All seemed well until July 1874, when Colonel George Armstrong Custer led a 7th Cavalry expedition through the Black Hills to establish an army post and to see if rumors of gold were true. Two of Custer's troops did discover gold while panning in French Creek, near present-day Custer in the southern hills. Word of the find leaked out, and white settlers moved in quickly. In accordance with the 1868 treaty, the military removed or arrested members of the first groups of settlers, including the 28 who spent the entire winter of 1874–75 at the "Gordon Stockade," a stockade the settlers had built for themselves in a remote area.

Despite threats from both the military and the Native Americans, miners continued to infiltrate the southern hills, and then they began moving north. Softening on its enforcement of the treaty, the military turned a blind eye to the intruders, who were violating the laws of the land. By Christmas 1874, a group of 20 miners had set up camp in Deadwood Gulch, where they had just found gold. Within months, thousands were living in "Deadwood," appropriately named for all the dead trees on the surrounding steep slopes. Some of the newcomers came to mine the mines, but many came to mine the miners. Supplies were needed, as were freighters to haul them in and bankers to handle the money; equally welcomed were some less respectable businesses like brothels, saloons, and gambling halls. Deadwood rapidly changed from a tent city to a real town. By September 1876, more than 200 permanent buildings had been built.

To understand just how much wealth tempted the fortune seekers, consider that in June and July of that year 50,000 ounces of gold, worth more than $1 million even at 1876 prices, was taken from the ground. Most of that gold came from the Homestake Mine, which was to eventually account for 10 percent of the gold mined in America. From 1876, when gold was first mined there, the Homestake ran continuously for 125 years, until it finally closed at the end of 2001.

**Last Sun to Deadwood,
Boulder Canyon,
South Dakota, 1994**

You could always sense something special about Boulder Canyon. I spent a lot of time waiting along its road from Sturgis to Deadwood, making photographs of bikes as they rode through its sharp turns, came over quick rises, slipped into its dips. I was shocked several years ago to find major construction going on. They scraped away the rises I loved so much, filled in the dips, smoothed out the turns. A wide path was cut through the forest so a modern four-lane highway could safely race gamblers to the new gaming halls of Deadwood, saving them minutes of precious time.

Flying Hair,
Interstate 90 Eastbound,
South Dakota, 1984

So what about the Native Americans and the Fort Laramie Treaty during this period? Understandably, the native people protested the incursions and sought to protect themselves and their lands. The government response was to stop enforcing the ban on non-Indians in the hills and to send a treaty commission to negotiate the purchase of the Black Hills in early December 1875. The commissioners, however, failed in their efforts. Following this unsuccessful transaction, the Commissioner of Indian Affairs issued an ultimatum stating that every Lakota not on the Great Sioux Reservation had to return there by January 31, 1876. This was an impossible demand, considering that most Sioux had never even heard of the ultimatum before its deadline, and even if they had, it would have been impossible for them to return to the reservation in winter conditions. The stage was set for the military to launch a campaign against the Sioux, who at the time were mostly living south of the Black Hills in northeastern Wyoming. The Sioux had joined forces with the Cheyenne. Together, they came under the leadership of Crazy Horse.

Tensions ran high. The deadline for returning to the reservation had passed. The U.S. government broke more of its promises to the Native Americans regarding food and clothing. A number of skirmishes broke out that spring. The most important were the Battle of the Rosebud, at which General George Crook was routed, and the much more famous Battle of the Little Big Horn in nearby Montana, which took Custer's life, along with the lives of 196 of his men. This last incident so outraged the American public, most of whom found out about it just in time for the Centennial Independence Day celebration eight days later, that the government had no problem gaining support to send much larger numbers of troops into the hills.

Within months, the remaining reservation leaders signed a new treaty which ceded the Black Hills. Most of the leaders and participants in the recent battles were on the run, and their sacred lands were lost forever. The battle was basically over, yet sporadic fighting continued. Crazy Horse didn't surrender until 1878 (after which he was killed by a bayonet wound inflicted by a soldier while he was imprisoned). In actuality, within a year of the Battle of the Little Big Horn, whites had taken complete control of the Black Hills, and the Native Americans had been pushed out and onto their meager reservations. So much for treaties!

Death of the Buffalo

Another even more insidious force was operating against the Native Americans during this period. For all time, they had depended on the buffalo for sustenance. Every part of the animal was used: buffalo chips served as fuel; internal organs became water vessels; horns were used as ladles and spoons; bones became knives, implement handles, and awls and needles for sewing; and skins provided material for clothing and teepee covers. Keep in mind that the buffalo population in North America at the beginning of the nineteenth century was estimated to number 60 million. It is believed that the Native Americans killed less than one-third of the number born in a year. It seemed the perfect relationship, but General Sheridan had another idea. He convinced President Grant that slaughtering the buffalo to eliminate the Native American's means of survival would solve the "Indian problem" more effectively than the army could. President Grant obviously agreed with Sheridan—he vetoed a congressional bill that had come before him to protect the buffalo.

A number of other factors came together in the 1870s that also helped bring about Sheridan's buffalo plan for controlling the Native Americans. A new tanning process made tanning buffalo hides more profitable; the railroad's western expansion split the herd and created a demand for buffalo meat to feed railroad building crews; and a public demand for more beef put the Texas Longhorn in direct competition with the buffalo for grazing lands.

The numbers tell the rest of the story. Millions of buffalo were killed between 1868 and 1881. Buffalo Bill Cody may be the most famous of the buffalo hunters, but he actually killed "only" 4,280 during the 18-month period that he was employed to help feed 1,200 construction workers of the Kansas Pacific railroad. By comparison, in one 60-day period in

Riding to the
Buffalo Chip, Sturgis,
South Dakota, 1993

1876, hunter Brick Bond killed a staggering 5,855 buffalo, including a one-day record of 300. Jim Cator was personally responsible for killing an average of 4,000 per year between 1872 and 1875. Although these men were record holders, so much slaughter was going on that the proud species was reduced to fewer than 500 survivors by 1885. The Brooklyn Zoo actually sent buffalo back west to help repopulate and save the species. President Cleveland eventually signed a bill to protect the species from total extinction. Too late, the public understood the magnitude of the damage wrought upon the buffalo. Unfortunately for the Native Americans, they were exactly where the U.S. government wanted them: on reservations, dependent on the government for their food and supplies.

With the invasion of white settlers, the Black Hills thrived, and so did the surrounding areas. Towns sprang up, and by 1878 a location for a military fort was finally selected. The fort was to be at the edge of the hills, just two miles from the mouth of Boulder Canyon, where stagecoaches from the Bismarck Trail, Sydney Trail, and Fort Pierre Trail all converged. Named Fort Meade, it was to be the home of the 7th Cavalry. Once the fort's location was decided, it was thought there should be a town nearby, closer than Deadwood, to serve it. A townsite company that included the fort commander, U.S. Army General Samuel D. Sturgis, was formed. It wasn't long before eighty acres of level ground were platted for a town, which was named Sturgis after the general. The town became a trading center, mostly supplying the fort with food and supplies, but it also became a center for the flat half of Lawrence County, where residents relied on ranching for their livelihood. Saloons and brothels opened, and the soldiers no longer felt the need to make the 14-mile trek to Deadwood. They could just follow Lazelle, the path named for Fort Mead's Major Henry Lazelle, right into Sturgis.

The town grew slowly until 1883. When a major flood destroyed much of Deadwood, Sturgis nearly doubled its population in one year due to the influx of refugees. In 1889, the same year South Dakota received statehood, Lawrence County was split in half, separating the mining interests from ranching. Deadwood remained the county seat of Lawrence County, and Sturgis became the county seat of the newly formed Meade County. Sturgis began to focus more on ranchers than miners at this point. Of course the town was still economically dependent on Fort Meade, which provided the ranchers with a market for their beef and horses. Loggers sold their wood to the residents of the fort, the iceman sold his ice to them, and the saloons and brothels depended on the soldiers for their business.

Over the ensuing decades, the justification for Fort Meade's existence repeatedly came into question. After the massacre at Wounded Knee in 1890, at which many of Fort Meade's soldiers were present, the "Indian problem" was finally settled. The need for a cavalry post to guard against possible attacks was difficult to defend. Despite this, community leaders were successful for the next few decades in lobbying to keep the post running. Legislators would

Still Downtown, Sturgis, South Dakota, 1984

repeatedly allocate funds for improvements to the post's buildings, water system, and other facilities. Then each time it came before Congress to close smaller posts like Fort Meade to support the army's policy of consolidation, it was argued that too much money had been recently spent on improvements.

It wasn't until 1943 that the city was assured that Fort Meade could remain a large part of the Sturgis economy, but this was only when the fort was finally decommissioned as an army post. In September 1944, after an interagency transfer was approved by President Roosevelt and after Congress signed off, Fort Meade was converted to one of nine Veterans Administration special hospitals, which were

being built to specialize in neuropsychiatry for the needs of veterans just coming out of the war. Then, almost 30 years later, the hospital's mission changed to make the facility a more general medical and surgical facility for veterans, which helped Sturgis to grow even more. By 1990, the hospital had a budget of $25 million, which made it an indispensable part of the local economy. In addition, parts of the facility were being used by the National Guard and by the Old Fort Meade Museum. It is a wonder of adaptation that this old cavalry post, which is so steeped in our nation's history, could so easily change from cavalry horses on the parade grounds to cavalry motorcycles, and barracks to hospital wards. Not only would there not have been a Sturgis had the fort never existed, the world also would have never seen a Black Hills Rally.

Seventies Portrait, Sturgis, South Dakota, 1981

No designer shades, no mirrors, just a simpler smile, a simpler place, a simpler time. Shared glances, hanging out with an arm around a waist, a small club. Were we happier?

Iron Horses in the Hills

Certainly, many factors contributed to the Black Hills Rally getting started, but most would agree it would not have launched had it not been for the efforts of local Sturgis resident John Clarence "Pappy" Hoel. Pappy was born in Sturgis to a family in the ice business. Originally, they cut the ice by hand from a pond that they had created on their land in Vannocker Canyon outside of Sturgis, then hauled it on horse-drawn wagons to their icehouse in Sturgis. Later, a motorized cutter was used, and trucks replaced the horse and wagons. Like many Sturgis residents, Pappy's family business depended on Fort Meade.

Pappy grew up working in the business and eventually took it over in the 1930s, but not long thereafter, it became obvious the business could not survive the coming of electric refrigeration. Having a longstanding interest in motorcycles, Pappy decided that selling them would be his new career. Harley-Davidson already had a dealer in nearby Rapid City, so Pappy successfully applied to establish an authorized Indian Motorcycle dealership in 1936. That same

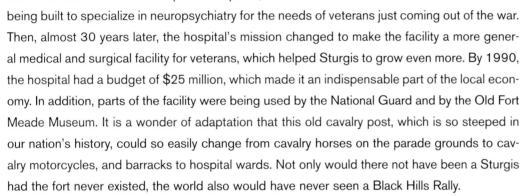

Heading South on Highway 85, Black Hills, South Dakota, 1999

Sunday morning, heading through the hills for the last time this bike week. It is brisk out, and you fall in and out of packs of other bikers heading home the same way. Climbing into the hills, the cool morning air is energizing. South of Deadwood, the road opens up into sweeping curves. Rhythmically, you rock back and forth, accelerating out of each turn. Moving forward, you know where you are going, but at the same time, you are lost in the wonderful journey.

year, he and a group of friends started a motorcycle club that was at first nameless. While out riding in the nearby hills, they pulled over for a rest. A car pulled up, and someone in the car hollered out that the group looked like a band of gypsies. They thought this was a great name, especially when combined with the name of the trees that surrounded them. They were known forever after as the Jackpine Gypsies.

Pappy's motorcycle shop became a nexus for the Gypsies, a place where they could gather and plan events. They rode their cycles all year long, even ice racing on Bear Butte Lake. In 1937, they organized races for clubs in the area. Then, at a meeting in early 1938, Pappy and his friends started to think bigger. They wondered why Sturgis couldn't have an event like Deadwood's "Days of '76 Rodeo" or Belle Fourche's "Black Hills Roundup Rodeo." Annual motorcycle races at the old abandoned half-mile track at the fairgrounds seemed like a great idea. After brainstorming, they promptly left the meeting to go over to Main Street to ask for the support of local business owners. Coming back with commitment for $500 in prize money, The Black Hills Motor Classic was born.

Before any races could be held, extensive repair work was needed to get Sturgis' old half-mile track back into proper condition. Jackpine Gypsy members threw themselves into clearing, cleaning, and leveling. They also needed to spread the word quickly, as that first rally and races were scheduled for August 14, 1938. Pappy helped publicize the rally by mounting signs on a converted sidecar rig attached to his Indian motorcycle, which he rode around the Black Hills to all of the events in the area. To be certain that he would be noticed, he modified the rig so it could carry Topsy, his Shetland pony. This motorcycle, sidecar, and pony combination developed quite a reputation at area parades and rodeos.

The first year's racing event was considered a huge success, with an estimated 175 people in attendance. Most of them slept in the Hoel's backyard, where a rented circus tent was set up to accommodate them. A tour through the Black Hills was planned for the first morning of the rally, before the races were to start. Pappy's wife, Pearl, with the help of a friend, made lunches for all the attendees and took them to a picnic area in Custer State Park while everyone else rode their bikes to Mount Rushmore.

You can say the rest is history, but it is still amazing to think that only a few decades ago Sturgis wasn't much more than a little known town on the edge of the northern Black Hills, where small town values came before fads or trends. In many respects, Sturgis is still that

20

small town on the edge of the Black Hills, but it is now known the world over. The Black Hills Rally put it on the map. It's doubtful that any member of the Jackpine Gypsies Motorcycle Club could have envisioned that the simple races they started in 1938 would lead to a motorcycle rally the scope of today's Sturgis. For one 10-day period each year, the town of 6,700 explodes to become the largest town in South Dakota. It boggles the mind to consider that the state capital, Pierre, has fewer than 13,000 citizens and the whole state of South Dakota has only 750,000. The rally attracted a record 600,000 visitors for the 60th anniversary rally in 2000! The way it has been growing, it won't be long before the number of attendees at the rally will double the population of the state.

The Rally Grows

When I first started riding a Harley-Davidson in the 1970s, the Sturgis rally was relatively small by today's standards. Still, it created quite a stir. It wasn't until 1978 that I made my first attempt to experience it. We didn't finish putting my 1971 Harley-Davidson Superglide back together until just after the rally was over that year, but if the event was as big as everyone said it was, I figured there would be something still going on one week later. I was wrong. As I rode through Sturgis, I never saw another motorcycle. This was a perfect opportunity for me to keep on going and going. So I rode up through the Dakotas, over to Michigan, into Canada and down the East Coast. It wasn't until the following year that I made it to the rally, on time for the Friday night party.

Visitors to Sturgis numbered in the thousands in the late 1970s. The sight of all the bikes parked in four neat rows down Main Street—there were photos that just had to be taken. As far as you could see, a dazzling array of chrome and enamel shone in the brilliant South Dakota sun. The proud owners of these machines, their faces filled with character, were not far off. I was amazed that so many people could share a common interest. The rally offered organized events like tours of the hills, flat track racing, and a hill climb put on by the same Jackpine Gypsies Motorcycle Club that had founded the rally, but most of the people I saw were like me, not there for any organized events. We came to be with other like-minded people. We came to ride the hills, to share two-wheeled tales over a drink, and to head out of town to catch some grudge racing near Bear Butte. We came to camp and party in City Park on the east edge of town. With the exception of the hill climb, several years went by before I attended anything listed on an official calendar. Actually, it was several years before I ever saw an official calendar.

Hot Town, Summer in the City, Sturgis, South Dakota, 1990

The 50th rally in 1990 was so hot that tar was oozing out of the street pavement. My boot soles adhered to the surface like suction cups and a Lovin' Spoonful song from 1966 played on repeat in my mind all week.

The party seemed to be centered in City Park, which was clearly the best place to camp. There were no fancy RVs and hookups in this campground—a pup tent seemed to be standard issue. I pitched mine in the back corner where the rest of the Boulder, Colorado, contingent was camped, but there were bikers from Los Angeles to Laconia nearby, characters with wonderful stories and interesting pasts, just wanting to be themselves and have a great time. How can you forget names like Bull, Half-Breed, Big Mouse, Sunshine, Little Mouse, Fat Albert, Little Pete, Big Pete, Mr. Tramp, Schultz, and Magoo? The bikes, too, wanted to just be themselves. The occasional British or Japanese bike, sometimes chopped in the style of the day, appeared, but mostly it was just old Harleys. The Evolution motors had not evolved yet; they were still a few years away. But the Harley engines had great names—Flathead, Knucklehead, Panhead, and Shovelhead. The faces and the bikes had no pretense, and I had no preconceptions. I photo-graphed it all, etching the faces, the bikes, and the attitude into my mind's eye.

A great group of bikers from Idaho camped with us. Knucklehead Company was nearby with their old Harley-Davidsons still running. A few sites away were Donnie and Happy Smith, who were still partners in Smith Brothers and Fetrow in Minneapolis. Of course, Donnie went on to achieve fame as a world-class custom bike builder, who has even made it into the Motorcycle Hall of Fame. Many others went on to make motorcycling the focus, even their livelihood, for the rest of their lives. My friend Charlie St. Clare became the executive director of the Laconia Motorcycle Rally and Race Week, while others like Smitty and Puppy opened bike shops—Smitty's in Florida and Puppy's in Mississippi. With a camera as an introduction, I got to meet these people and many more, forming friendships that continue to this day.

**Up in Flames,
City Park, Sturgis,
South Dakota, 1982**

The city might have closed the City Park anyway but burning the Port-O-Potties nailed the lid on the coffin. When the city council met the following month, a resolution passed to close the park gates to rally campers forevermore.

The town of Sturgis was responsible for opening the park to camping and eventually for closing it as well. The town charged a few dollars per person to cover basic services, but that seemed to be as far as the city got involved. Once inside the gate there were few rules other than those with which we governed ourselves. We made our own fun. There were late night campfires, two-up drag racing down narrow asphalt paths between crowds and tents, mud wrestling in Bear Butte Creek, and impromptu wet-T competitions supported by a passed hat. Some citizens lined Lazelle with binoculars in hopes of catching a glimpse while others lobbied the city to shut the park down for the immoral behavior they knew was going on within the its gates. For the most part, the goings on were harmless, but there were occasional accidents. Funny enough, it was the torching of the homemade Port-A-Pottys in 1982 (out of protest that they weren't being cleaned often enough) that gave the city its excuse to close the park to camping forever. It was the end of an era.

The closing of City Park prompted all sorts of changes. Opportunities abounded. Privately owned campgrounds grew and new ones opened up. Glencoe and the Buffalo Chip campgrounds, the two biggest campgrounds, both opened their gates at that time. The rally developed commercially throughout the 1980s, with big-name concerts, new bars, venues, and businesses that catered to motorcyclists. The types of bikers who started coming to the rally was changing too. It was during this period that it became okay to have a good career and a lot of money and ride a Harley as well. I believe Malcolm Forbes was largely responsible for bringing about this change in attitude as he took his friends and his Harleys on tours all around the world. Lawyers, doctors, investment bankers, and other professionals began to ride and attend the rally. Malcolm made it as well in 1987 with his entourage of "Capitalist Tools" (the group of red-vested friends he rode with), his Boeing 727 jet plane, and his Harley-Davidson Softail-shaped hot air balloon.

As more bikers came to Sturgis, more tourists came to watch. The look and feel of Main Street was changing. Many businesses realized they could make far more money with a short-term lease to a biker-run out-of-town business than by staying open during the rally. Some found it not worth staying open the rest of the year. Sturgis' economy was making adjustments as it had in the past to support the cavalry post and the ranching community. In hindsight, it seems it was all part of a grand plan to get ready for the 50th celebration that was approaching in 1990. How else could the crowds have been handled?

Meanwhile, Harley-Davidson had its own plans. As it maneuvered through the 1980s from near bankruptcy to meteoric growth, popularity, and a stock offering, it changed its relationship with Sturgis. First, Harley moved its rally headquarters from the Sturgis Super-8 motel to Rapid City, which offered more accommodations, restaurants, and a large venue to host its trade show. The little parking lot that once hosted its ride-in show could no longer support its needs nor, perhaps, its image. Harley-Davidson was too big for Sturgis, and I felt betrayed by its departure. At first, I stayed away from the new venue. How could Harley-Davidson abandon Sturgis? But in true Harley fashion, the Motor Company proved itself right. The small town on the edge of the hills could no longer support what the rally was becoming. Sturgis, the town, had city limits. Sturgis, as an idea, had no limits.

Malcolm Forbes
and Liz Taylor,
New Jersey, 1987

Malcolm's Softail Balloon
Flying in Sturgis,
South Dakota, 1987

23

ILFORD XP2   1854

**Rainbow, Sundance,
Wyoming, 1999**

Dark skies above. Under the bridge,
voices wait out the storm. Sharing
stories, staying dry, becoming
friends. I play my whistle as shapes
come into frame, a rainbow tying
them together. It is magic.

The 50th Anniversary

By the late 1980s, motorcycling had become more popular than ever. Bike registrations were increasing and more people were on the roads on two wheels. A rumbling began as to how big the 50th anniversary celebration was going to be. By 1989, at the 49th rally, the rumbling became a roar: Bikers shared a certainty that this anniversary was going to be something that shouldn't be missed, an event that would go down in history. Reservations were booked a year in advance. Anyone who had ever been to the rally made plans to go back for the 50th. Anyone who hadn't been there before didn't want to miss it. Even with all the talk and hype in the media, I don't think anyone could have predicted how large the rally would turn out to be. The number of visitors, hitting the 400,000 mark, was staggering. Members of large and small bike clubs showed up in the hundreds. Music, sports, and film celebrities made the scene. There were long lines for everything, from getting a beer to finding a table in a restaurant to even going to the bathroom. Traffic on Interstate 90 was backed up for miles, in a part of the country that had only heard the term *traffic jam* used with reference to cities like Chicago and Los Angeles.

After this celebration, the rally was never the same. While the 50th set all sorts of records, rally statistics never dropped back to those from prior years. As for the rest of the motorcycle world, registrations continued to climb and the industry grew to support them. Harley-Davidsons began appearing in films, television, commercials, and print ads for other products. Actors, actresses, and musicians would often be shown on or with their Harleys. Harley-Davidson just kept cashing in on the publicity.

I believe that as daily life in America began to move even faster and become more complex, increasingly shaped by technology and commerce, people were looking for a "great escape." Motorcycling was there for them, with Sturgis ready in the wings. You could be blue collar, white collar, or no collar—it didn't matter. You just had to don your leathers, hit the road and feel the wind in your face. Riding a bike could make you feel, at least for that moment, that you were different, a nonconformist, without a routine. No cares or worries to bother you. Neither boss nor "Big Brother" watching.

Many bikers today just pass through the town of Sturgis for a day or two as part of their annual two-week, two-wheeled western sojourn, while others may only stop for a few hours. They come from farther and farther away and as they do, they seem to stay longer. The weekend before the rally officially starts has become bigger than the final weekend, when the campgrounds have emptied, their occupants already on their long journeys home. While at the rally, bikers explore what is in the hills as well as the plains surrounding them. They make tours of the Badlands or ride to Devil's Tower, and they ride through the northern hills as well as the southern. But everyone, from scooter tramp to R.U.B. (Rich Urban Biker) pays homage to Sturgis, the birthplace of the rally. The town has been called "motorcycle mecca," an appropriate title considering the dictionary defines "mecca" as "a place that is an important center for a particular activity or that is visited by a great many people."

Watching new visitors get their first glimpses of Sturgis' Main Street, you can see the *Wow* in their faces. There is nothing like this anywhere. Our experiences and interpretations of Sturgis are as different as one person is from the next. Some are taken aback by the scope and scale of what is before them. For others, it is the details—the strange things that may be sold nowhere else on the planet, the funny pins and patches, the unique clothing, and occasionally the lack of clothing. Sturgis has bikes with two engines, bikes with three seats, bikes that almost sit on the ground, and others that must ride like tanks. Some bikes are spray painted with cans of orange or black paint, and others have ten clear coats of lacquer over skulls

and dragons. There is something for everyone but for me, first and foremost, there are those fascinating faces. Old, weathered faces divulge lifetimes of experiences, and beautiful young faces hunger to have the experiences. Some faces are covered with tattoos, and others are hidden by masks. And with each face are countless stories.

To contrast the *Wow* side of Sturgis, there is the quiet side. Could there be a quiet side to Sturgis, you ask? Think of the feeling you get when you ride down a winding two-lane road in the hills. The sun is low on the horizon and you are by yourself, or perhaps you are with some close friends who share the experience. The V-twin is firing away beneath you, yet somehow this is quiet. This is peace. This is freedom. Some people go to places of worship for the same experience. They go there to break their daily routines and stir their senses. They go to contemplate and awaken their consciousness. They go to be close to friends and neighbors. Could there be a similarity?

This is how I feel when I am out riding my Harley at those magic times. The feeling may be even more powerful riding outside the hills, particularly east of Sturgis, with tall prairie grass to both sides and the large mound of igneous rock we call Bear Butte rising from the horizon. For me, as for many bikers, this misnamed landmark (for it is not a flat-topped butte at all) symbolizes Sturgis. The Plains Indian name of "Mato Paha," or "Sacred Mountain" is much more appropriate. I believe the Native Americans are right about it being sacred, because you can sense something special about it when you see its strong shape rise up from the flat plain below or as you come near to it. Maybe this is why each year bikers are married on its slopes and Native Americans tie prayer cloths to so many of its trees. They still visit the site to fast, to pray, and to achieve their vision quests. After more than 20 years of participating in and photographing the rally, I have seen it change just as I have seen myself change. I was younger and wilder, just as the rally was. We were both naive and a little less worldly. The town outgrew its geographic boundaries years ago, so that it is no longer a town; it is a phenomenon. It is a feeling inside. It is still a destination, but it has come to represent the journey. It stands for all that motorcycling is, for all that motorcycling can be. This collection of photographs is my interpretation of Sturgis. While many of the images are the result of serendipity, most are the result of a more conscious effort. Combined, they represent my experience of Sturgis. Perhaps after viewing these images through your own experience, you will see for yourself that Sturgis is really just your own unique state of mind.

**Backdrop,
South of Nemo,
South Dakota, 1997**

It was as if my handlebars were clamped to a studio stand in front of a painted backdrop, only I was cruising at speed down a beautiful highway south of Nemo. No scouting, no staging, no re-shoots—this is riding in the hills.

**Needles Highway Slot,
South Dakota, 2000**

During the Rally, the Black Hills are
black with Harleys. The bikes
become part of the scenery. I ride
the steep, windy roads and pull
over repeatedly to scamper up
embankments, crawl into ditches or
straddle double yellow lines, all in
hopes that a pack, or perhaps a
single bike will come through the
tunnel, across the bridge or into the
rocky slot to complete my vision.

THE ROAD

Puppy and Bear Butte, Sturgis, South Dakota, 1994

This shot was taken in 1994 while I was shooting a feature on Puppy's 1937 Harley-Davidson Flathead in Sturgis. Since we were near Bear Butte, we slipped out to grab a few frames while the light was good.

I have photographed Puppy performing this feat several times since we met in the late '70s. I have actually photographed quite a few people doing this same thing, but in this frame Puppy seems to exude the spirit of what biking is all about more than any other similar shot I have taken. A friend of mine wrote a headline for Puppy that captures that spirit: "Feel the Freedom."

Born to Be Wild, Riding East of Sturgis, South Dakota, 1992

Some people were born to be wild. While I don't know Jimmy very well, I've seen him ride for many years and he's the best. It doesn't take much for him to get out in front of the bar, one on one, to see who's fastest in Beulah, Wyoming. Or anywhere else. He is one with the bike when he is out there. This is one of the few shots I have of him where he's not out grudge racing, yet it is all Jimmy.

Backlit Pack, Sturgis, South Dakota, 1996

Riding with Senator Campbell, Sturgis, South Dakota, 1996

Senator Ben Nighthorse Campbell has always been a big supporter of motorcycles and biker rights. He is often spotted riding through traffic in Washington, D.C., on his Harley-Davidson, but I believe he would rather be riding around Sturgis or near his ranch in southern Colorado. When and where he can, he helps bikers in a variety of ways including his efforts to make the Four Corners Iron Horse Rally a major bike event. Obviously, he has a great spirit and is open to new ideas, even when those ideas land him on a small rigid chopper flying through the hills.

Flying the Flag, Interstate 90 near
Rapid City, South Dakota, 1994

Coming At You, Wyoming, 1994

"When I was 16, I was going to jail and the judge said, 'Jail or service boy,' so I went in the service. And I fucked up there, too. Steady.

I got an honorable discharge, but by the skin of my teeth. I stayed in trouble the whole time I was in the service and I rode my motorcycle.

And in May of '64, I bought this 1937 flathead that I've ridden all these years. I took my first road trip within six months of getting it together.

And I ended up in jail. And it got stolen and I got it back. A little bit at a time. A piece here and there. Some of it I never got back. Some of it

they took a hammer to. I took some flywheels out of a kid's bike in Fort Hood, Texas and I left his bike on the side of the road; and the flywheels

he got stolen (were) from me. I put it back together and have ridden it pretty much ever since. I rode with a couple of clubs. I rode around the

United States every year. And I'm not sure, but I think that basically my first thing was to be a rebel."

−From an interview with Puppy, Sturgis, 1991

**Wyoming Sea, Wyoming,
1997**

The ground swells like waves
on the sea, undulating under
a vast western sky. Motorcycles
move through it in formation.
It is endless.

Riding Alongside Mr. Tramp, Sturgis, South Dakota, 1982

"I think Mr. Tramp was the first real scooter tramp. He was a one-of-a-kind character, that's for damn sure. Absolutely everybody he met loved him. He was a biker, a tattoo artist, and lady's man. He was always on his motorcycle, and he always had a collection of fine women around him. He even died on his motorcycle when a guy hit him just after Christmas, in the dead of winter, in the mid-1980s."

—Billy Tinney, *Easyriders* Photographer and
Editor of *Tattoo* magazine, 2003

The One and Only, Sturgis, South Dakota, 2001

"There was never anyone like George before, and there will never be anyone like him again.

He was one of the few guys you meet in life that becomes the one and only of his type.

George really had two lives, one from before he went to prison (he served 9 years), and one after

he got out. After he got out, he appreciated life so much more. And he loved motorcycles

because that was his way of realizing he was free of the bars that locked him up. It was riding

and partying that meant everything to George. He out-rode the riders, he out-partied the partiers."

George Jupin, R.I.P. May 25, 1962–January 21, 2003

—From Billy Lane and Nick Fredella, 2003

Unique Waterbeds, Interstate-90, Wyoming, 1984

In the 1970s and early 1980s, waterbeds were everywhere, just like the Shovelheads we all rode.

My waterbed burst. My Shovelhead is still running.

Maverick Junction, South Dakota, 1999

Truck stops and cafés are often the best way to remember our travels. The journey itself can blend together
in a swirl of images, but somehow the truck stop is frozen in time. Not a soul in sight as I put four gallons in the tank.
I park and go in for a drink or a meal. I get the flavor of the land from the inflection of the waitress' voice and
the subtle variations in the standard menu.

Like a Rolling Stone, Lusk, Wyoming, 1982

**Sons' and Iron Horsemen Camp Near Bear Butte,
Sturgis, South Dakota, 1997**

While Fort Meade was being built south of this location in 1878, the 7th Cavalry camped
west of Bear Butte not far from where this photo was taken at a site named Camp Sturgis. In times
past, alongside their ponies in the prairie grass, soldiers in uniform must have made ready for games
of strength and horsemanship just to pass the time.

Kai and Devil's Tower, Wyoming, 2002

Even though Kai comes from South Dakota, this was his first time to the "Tower"
and his best ever riding day in Sturgis. It is great to see guys his age building twisted choppers.
Fresh ideas are brewing in a whole new generation.

3017 ILFORD XP2 SUPER

46

Sunset Strip, Wyoming, 1999

The sun is beginning to fade. There is a chill, then it returns to create long shadows. The bikes
move in and out, changing position. They flow through this western expanse, fluid as they
dance across the highway.

Bikes Across the Plains, Wyoming, 1999

The plains glisten in the bright western sun while bikes and dotted lines converge between
the distant landscape and the "Stonehenge" shadow of an interstate overpass.

Day Trippers,
Wyoming Wednesday,
1998

Flying through Wyoming, 2002

"Riding in Wyoming is wide open. You want to go fast and go forever and you don't want to stop.
Then to get a girl to say, 'I'll get on with you, I don't care what I'm sitting on or where my feet are,
I'm with you.' Riding like that is almost like having sex."

—Billy Lane, 2003

Rolling into the Hills, Wyoming, 1992

This is the landscape of northeastern Wyoming, the area that leads you into the Black Hills.
The roads roll over gentle countryside covered with wildflowers. It makes for great riding.
The tendency is to go fast, but there can be a little deception in the beauty. I've been nicked
for speeding twice as I've come over one of these tempting rollers only to receive
a formal greeting from the "Law."

Me and My Shadow, Interstate-25, Wyoming, 2002

Grass, sky, pavement. Etched by the harsh light, simple shapes and forms create
a western landscape. As my shadow grows tall, we are alone, just the two of us.

Yellow Frame,
Boulder Canyon, Sturgis,
South Dakota, 1986

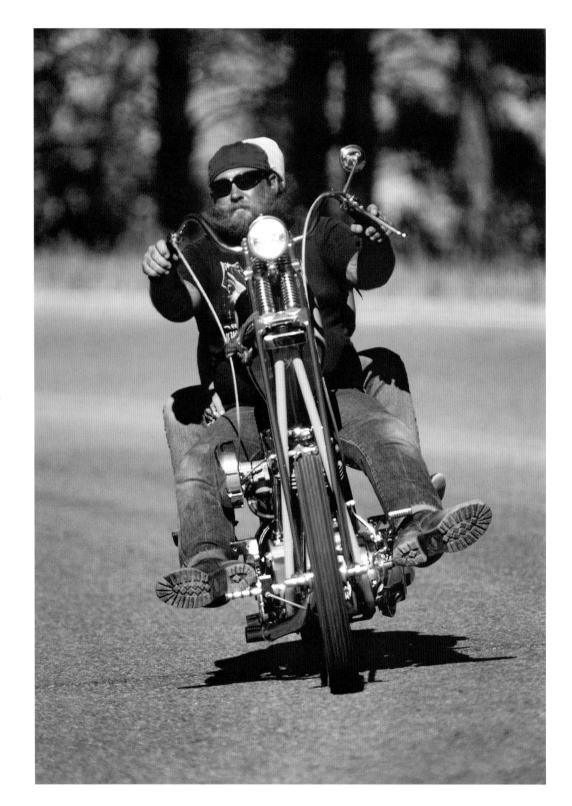

Riding Back to Sturgis, Wyoming, 1997

I lived with this couple for several years. I live with all the people in my photographs.

Looking at the images over and over again, it is easy to make up stories about who they are,

where they come from, and what they do. I know this couple well now.

Someday, I hope to meet them.

Riding the Back Roads, East of Sturgis, South Dakota, 1995

After I finished shooting a pictorial about a group of bikes built by Don Hotop, he and his friends set
off for Sturgis. I imagine crossing America looked this way in 1910, when Harley-Davidson
was seven years old and the word *travel* was synonymous with adventure.

Ghost Rider, Sturgis Bound, Colorado, 1981

Sometimes, when you are out riding alone, you find yourself joining up with another rider without even knowing who they are or where they are going. I presume this person was heading to Sturgis as I was in 1981 but I'll never know for sure. I doubt he has any idea this photo exists. It is just a scribbled note about a moment in time. With a little nod, I pulled off for gas, as smoothly as when I pulled up alongside, never to know his identity.

Heat Cells Burn in Rain, Sturgis, South Dakota, 1982

As the Sturgis rally has grown in size and bikers come from farther away, the event has gotten longer.
The craziness that used to get concentrated into two or three days is now spread out over ten.
When people ask what Sturgis was like in the early '80s, I have a lot of stories to pick from or I can
sum it up by saying, "Heat Cells Burn in Rain."

Walk the Line, Sturgis, South Dakota, 1994

Where there are bikes, there is no shortage of police, even on roads that could go a year without seeing a cruiser. What is worse is that regardless of what you may be stopped for, you could end up with a potentially illegal search or inspection. The scene wasn't dissimilar when my own Harley was confiscated in 1979 for more than two years. These are conservative times. It is more important than ever to know your rights and protect your freedoms.

"Officer, please understand: I have the right to have an attorney present if you want to question me or conduct any search of my body or personal effects. I am not giving my consent to any type of search. If I am under arrest, I wish to invoke and exercise my Miranda Rights. I want to speak with an attorney now. I do not want my personal property impounded, nor do I consent to any impoundment. I request the opportunity to secure my personal effects. If I am not under arrest, please tell me immediately so that I may leave."

—From a popular wallet guide from attorney Richard M. Lester

Storm Rider, Riding North of Sturgis,

South Dakota, 1993

This torrential downpour burst on a Wednesday afternoon during a concert

at a ranch just north of Sturgis. Most people stayed put, hoping it would pass over quickly,

but others went for it. The rain turned to hail and it hurt. People see this and laugh

as they recall being caught like this, recall feeling like pins were piercing their face,

and recall the wet that went all the way through them.

It's anything but funny when you're in it.

After the Storm, Riding to the Drags,
Belle Fourche, South Dakota, 1980

In 1979, there were hill climbs and flat-track racing but there was no drag strip in Sturgis.

If you wanted to see Pete Hill on his Knuckle, you had to ride to Belle Fourche. It was

questionable whether they would be racing on this day as the group of mostly Boulder bikers

left Sturgis' City Park campground. Halfway to the track, the skies began to clear.

The rainbow appeared just as the sun made the wet pavement and prairie grasses glow.

Free spirits crossed the Great West.

61

FTW, Sturgis, South Dakota, 1981

Giving someone the finger like this in 1981 was a little outrageous, but I wasn't the focus
of any anger. This was just someone saying, "Fuck the World. I'm doing my own thing."

Perfect Ride, Sturgis, South Dakota, 1996

Riding at night after a long, hot day is the best. The afternoon sun was too strong and too intense,

but now it is just right. You follow the centerline down the road to the sound of your engine

beating rhythmically. It is hypnotic. Occasionally, the road may turn or the lights

of a car may startle you, but you go on not wanting it to end. Alone with your thoughts.

Alone on the Perfect Ride.

Wyoming Sunset Ride,

Riding Back to Sturgis, 1998

Two Minnesota women led this group back from Wyoming. The sun shone off their skin

as it set behind them. When you are on a motorcycle you are exposed to the elements and

sense every nuance of change. You feel the difference in temperature as you go over a stream

or the moisture as you ride past an irrigated field. Day turns to night almost unnoticed

in a car, but on a bike you shiver as the cold rips through your body. You feel alive.

You remember, forever.

THE FACES

Stylin' on Main, Sturgis,
South Dakota, 1987

Tattoo Window, Sturgis, South Dakota, 1984

"Crazy Ace was one of those people who put tattooing on the map. He was a pioneer. He was one of the first artists, along with Mr. Tramp, who set up in Sturgis. I owe him a lot. He always helped me out in the early days. There was always a place reserved for my studio in the back of his tattoo area somewhere on Main Street, and he would always have a whole lot of girls lined up ready to be photographed when I got there. He's still an infamous tattoo artist, and he's a biker. At one time, he had a motorcycle and tattoo shop in Richmond, Virginia. Then he started promoting some of the first tattoo conventions around. He worked here in the States for years but for now, as far as North America is concerned, Crazy Ace is staying well north of the border in Canada where he's a citizen."

—*Billy Tinney,* Easyriders *photographer and editor of* Tattoo *magazine, 2003*

**Late Night Around the Campfire, City Park,
Sturgis, South Dakota, 1979**

Late at night by the campfire, a bottle is passed. Time and the world beyond become a concept.
This is a chance to share stories and tales of the road. One by one, campers drift off, only a few
remain. Voices interrupt the quiet. Then silence as dawn breaks.

Property of Paul, Main Street, Sturgis, South Dakota, 1979

"When I first got my 'Property Of' buckle, I hated it. I wasn't going to wear it, so it hung on the back of my chair for three weeks. I got the impression that this guy thought he owned me and controlled me, but I knew I was a single, independent woman and I wasn't anybody's property. My man wasn't happy. I didn't understand that it meant more to him to give me that buckle than to give me a diamond ring. Eventually, I started getting to know more people and realized that if you wore the buckle, you were more respected by the brothers in the club. It also provides protection, to a certain degree, because people realize you are with a club and they leave you alone. I have been wearing my buckle for almost six years now. I feel naked without it. It's a part of me and I wear it with pride."

—Donna on "Property Of," 2003

The Place Your Mother Warned You About,
Sturgis, South Dakota, 1996

Sturgis *is* the place your mother warned you about. Maybe that is why everyone wants to come.
It is still about bikers but there are others—young coeds looking for a good time, musicians looking
for fame, and street people looking for a handout. Everyone is searching for their dream.

Zeke, Sturgis, South Dakota 1997

While a club brother was going through chemotherapy for bad cancer, Zeke shaved his head to let him
know he wasn't alone. It helped. The brother's negative and self-conscious attitude turned around.
His cancer went into remission, but unfortunately it came back. As I was on the telephone with
my editor finalizing the text for this book, I received a message on my computer saying I had an
incoming e-mail. I opened it up while still on the phone and read the following message:

"I am Jackie, TK's Ol' lady with Sons of Silence. Well, his widow. TK was in remission for a year after
your photo was taken, but then he got the cancer back and he died in October of 2001. It was
a long, hard road for TK for 7 years. I was there for all of it and to watch this strong tough man
become weak—it was very hard. It's still hard to think about it. It is nice that you are showing that
Bike Clubs aren't what they are put out to be in most people's eyes—uncaring. Sons of Silence are
very caring people, and I highly commend them and will be grateful to them 'til I die."

Zeke has since grown his hair back.

Wedding Dress, Sturgis, South Dakota, 1982

Harley riders are passionate. They are passionate about their bikes, about riding, about partying
and about their brothers and sisters. Riding in the wind and elements, so close to the edge,
they feel life all around them.

Street Portrait, Sturgis, South Dakota, 1987

Bea, Puppy's Pig Roast, Whitewood, South Dakota, 1991

"There's one thing you've got to learn out of life: You don't do anything they tell you to.
You do everything they tell you don't do. I did that for forty-one years and I had
a beautiful marriage. They'd tell me to do something and I'd tell them to go to hell.
Who the hell needs any electric start? I still use a kick-starter on that old '56 of mine,
if I ever get it together again.

"They told me I had cancer and they didn't expect me to live more than a year or two.
And I told them I was going to live forever way back in '66. And I'm still here.
I'll be here a long time after they're gone too."

—From an interview with Bea
at Puppy's house, August, 1991

High Bars at the Oasis,
Sturgis, South Dakota, 1987

Tattoo Parlor,
Sturgis, South Dakota, 1980

**Just Married, Sturgis,
South Dakota, 1994**

I have attended many biker
weddings, but at this wedding
I was just an innocent bystander
as the procession rode down
Main Street. It had already passed
me before I realized what was
going on, but all the elements came
together quickly in this one frame.

As people look at this photo,
they seem to enjoy the fact
that there are people out there as
unconventional as this couple
appears to be.

Masked Woman, Main Street, Sturgis, South Dakota, 1994

Main Street is intriguing. You never know what you may see. It is like a show,
but perhaps one you don't need to take the kids to. Can you help but wonder
what some of these people do the other 355 days a year?

Cowboys and Bikers, Sundance, Wyoming, 1994

Cowboys and bikers have always been connected in my mind. Owen Wister, the author of the classic western novel *The Virginian*, wrote about Wyoming in the 1880s and 1890s as it was changing before him. I thought of bikers as I read the book. The hero had all the attributes we associate with cowboys and bikers: honesty, courage, strength, and integrity. In the introduction to the book, written in 1902, he wrote, "What is to become of the horseman, the cowpuncher, the last romantic figure upon our soil? For he was romantic. Whatever he did, he did with his might. The bread that he earned was earned hard, the wages that he squandered were squandered hard . . . he will be here among us always, invisible, waiting his chance to live and play as he would like. His wild kind has been among us always, since the beginning: a young man with his temptations, a hero without wings."

Shit Happens,
Main Street, Sturgis,
South Dakota, 1987

Shovelhead in the Rain, Sturgis, South Dakota, 1987

Sharpshooter, Sturgis, South Dakota, 1987

"I met Joe Barcelona in 1984 in Deadwood when he was doing card tricks to get drinks
in the bars. He never had to buy a drink. We got to be good friends, and because he liked
a lot of us, he'd come around to the campground and do his quick draw and sharp-shooting for us.
He had a good time, and he'd drink a lot. Then he died in the mid 90s."

—JR (former Sons of Silence National President) 2003

Chattanooga Charlie, Sturgis, South Dakota, 1986

Chattanooga Charlie used to be a fixture on the streets of Sturgis during the rally.
Before his accident, he would bring a brand-new custom three-wheeler each year.
Later, he would just change the paint and make smaller modifications.

Charlie arrived on Main Street early each morning to get a good parking spot on the
south side of the street, midway between Junction and First. You could be assured
he would be sitting in his foldup chair on the shady side of the street, visiting with people,
telling stories with his Southern drawl, or showing off his photo album filled with pictures
of himself and the women who had posed topless beside him. If you were one of the lucky few,
you may have even tasted his moonshine.

Chatanooga Charlie is one of those characters who helped make the rally.
He died in the early 1990s.

Bandido and Child,
Sturgis, South Dakota,
1990

The Weasels MC, Wyoming, 1999

Unlike an outlaw motorcycle club, the "Weasels" came together, according to Kim Peterson, one of the founders, as a drinking club with a motorcycle problem. It grew from a small group in Agoura Hills, California, into a loose-knit organization of fun seekers. Its members can be found all across America as well as in Japan, Finland, Sweden, Denmark, Canada, Mexico, and Ireland. They're easy to spot, especially if you find yourself in a bar on a Wednesday night, the official Weasel drinking night ("Weasel Wednesday"). Look for a biker in a bright orange T-shirt, a weasel across the chest, and a drink in hand.

Everybody's Talking, Sturgis, South Dakota, 1991

Just for Fun, Sturgis, South Dakota, 1984

Faces, City Park, Sturgis, South Dakota, 1980

City Park was a world of its own, a protective sanctuary for many. Once inside its gates,

very little existed beyond. Such an odd collection of personalities, backgrounds, and faces.

Was this the heart of America in 1980?

Young Rider, Sturgis, South Dakota, 1991

Street Gawkers, Junction and Main,
Sturgis, South Dakota, 1991

Snakemouth, Sturgis, South Dakota, 1991

Street Talk, Sturgis, South Dakota, 1995

I love to watch people, especially when they seem animated and alive. It's during those moments that they seem like kids, forgetting they have dressed for a performance. They are just themselves.

Arm Wrestling, Sturgis, South Dakota, 1997

Clubs occasionally host games involving feats of strength or skill, like arm wrestling, battery tossing, beer chugging, knife throwing, or drag racing. At parties like this one, hosted by the Sons of Silence and the East Coast Iron Horsemen, prospects keep busy, but most everyone else is there just for fun. Members of the host clubs, as well as guest clubs, get to know each other, and the brotherhood stays tight. No need for expensive equipment or conventional etiquette. Muscle and brawn—it doesn't get any more basic than this.

Magoo, Main Street, Sturgis, South Dakota, 1997

When not at his North Dakota tattoo parlor, Magoo can be found at bike runs all
over the country working his tattoo art or just having fun. He travels with two little dogs that
fit inside his leather vest yet have the meanest growl you can imagine. Magoo lives the life.

Gold Tooth, Sturgis, South Dakota, 1996

**Tattooed Dog,
Sturgis, South Dakota,
1994**

People sense a photographer's
interest and are quick to show off.
There is usually something
interesting on the flipside.

Sportster Sunset, Sturgis, South Dakota, 1995

THE PLACE

The Lineup, Sturgis, South Dakota, 1993

I have always loved the compressed look of a line of custom bikes, their wonderful paint and convoluted chrome reflections when parked so close to each other. They are like raw materials waiting to be abstracted into color, shape, and form.

Artist Scott Jacobs and I discussed this image before he painted it as "Fork it Over." We talked about the qualities of the image that make it uniquely photographic and different from traditional painting, particularly the highly selective focus. Scott felt this would be the most challenging part of interpreting the photograph into paint. He did a fabulous job. Taken together, the painting and the photograph make me think of how photography has affected painting and painting has affected photography for more than 150 years.

Young Couple on Dresser, City Park, Sturgis, South Dakota, 1980

Early Morning, City Park, Sturgis, South Dakota, 1979

I arrived in Sturgis for my first rally too late to see the lay of the land, but just in time for the all-night party that happened every night in City Park. This was my first morning in Sturgis. I woke up, not having slept much, and assessed the damages both internally and externally. What sort of toll did the party take? There was drag racing down the narrow pavement between the tents, there were campfires, wildness until all hours of the morning, and a dreamlike recollection of police cars with lights flashing, screaming through the park in the middle of the night.

In the morning, it is quiet and peaceful.

Choppers at Junction and Main, Sturgis, South Dakota, 1979

Where is everybody? Is this really the busiest corner in Sturgis on Saturday, the biggest day
of the rally? Rossini went on to create his famous tattoo parlor in this barbershop, and this corner went
on to be the best corner for citizens, bikers, and the police to watch the scene. Though Rossini is
no longer with us—he died in early 2003—and you don't see Honda choppers like this anymore,
the long and low look is back today. Raked front ends, metal flake, pull-back bars. If we wait long
enough, any style is bound to return.

Bike Wash, Sturgis, South Dakota, 1984

Big Pete, Guy, and Marty, Near Sturgis, South Dakota, 1979

There was always someone whose bike wasn't running and they would drive the pick-up.

Call it what you will—beer truck, chase truck, grip truck—it was there when you needed it.

You didn't think much about pulling over on a hot day for a cold one.

The times sure have changed.

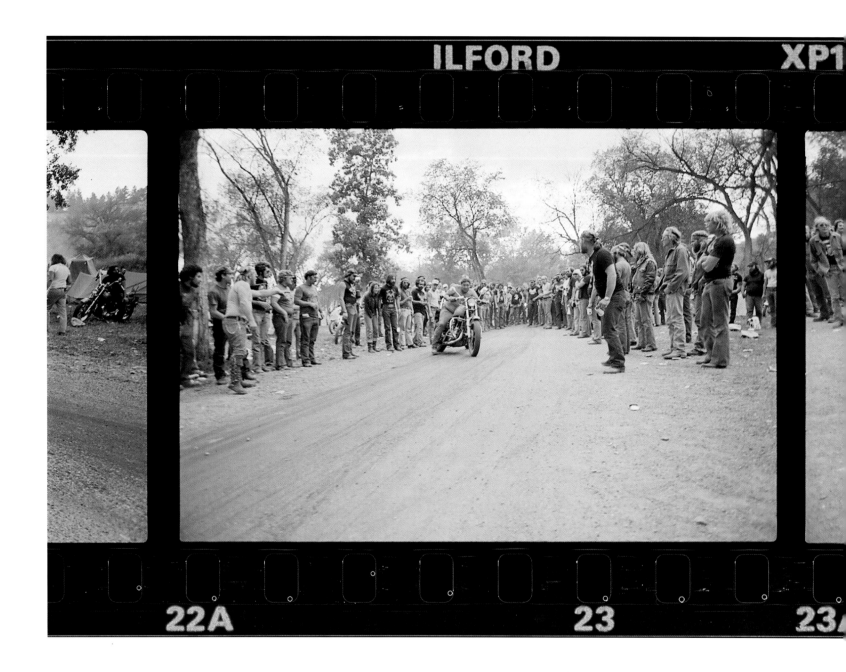

400

24   24

Crash, City Park, Sturgis, South Dakota, 1981

The hand-scribbled note on the back of my contact sheet to the editors read, "That bike's front tire hit me before it stopped!" That's what City Park was like. Not that it was out of control, but it was pretty close to the edge. And that's probably why we kept going back.

Harleys at the TT Races,
Jackpine Gypsies' Track,
Sturgis, South Dakota,
1994

Jackpine Gypsies' Hillclimb,
Sturgis, South Dakota, 1979

Drag Race Finals, Sturgis, South Dakota, 1999

The drags seem to be different than all other types of motorcycle racing. For one thing, people who say
they have no interest in motorcycle racing seem to love going to the drags. Even the bike clubs participate.
It's their chance to put their skill and machines on the line against other clubs.

Grudge Racing Near Bear Butte, Sturgis, South Dakota, 1980

Burning rubber racing to Bear Butte. Happy Smith watches. Crazy John still on his Honda.
No center line. A blown piston on a Sporty ends the fun. I survive a high-speed wobble racing
back to town. Did the 7th Cavalry make up games when they first came here and camped
near this very spot over 100 years ago?

Staging Before the Start, Sturgis, South Dakota, 1994

The area before the start where the drag bikes do their final preparations is the staging area.
I always liked the name because it reminds me of theatre. Everyone is in their precise position,
waiting for their cue.

Off the Line, Lori Dalton at the Drags, Sturgis, South Dakota, 1988

Lori's riding impressed me. There was something about the way she sat so nimbly on her
500-pound Harley-Davidson, feet barely touching the ground, eyes peering ahead as she waited
for the green light. Then with the crack of her wrist, she lifted the front end off the ground and drove
the power to the back tire, twisting and contorting it as it struggled to grip the asphalt and
propel her down the strip.

Eyes on the Start, Sturgis, South Dakota, 1996

"Once you get on the bike, it's like heaven. It's the best thing in the world. Once you sit on it, the rest of everything gets almost kind of quiet and goes away. I can do some pretty good burnouts. And I can hear the crowd over the bike sometimes when the burnouts goin'. Some guys are screamin' and yellin'. And that's pretty neat and you kind of chuckle, but you're inside that helmet and to me it's like being in my own little space. I can focus on that light. I don't know, but if you have to think about it you shouldn't be there. I don't race anyone else. That guy's not there. If he wants to race me, that's fine. But I'm going out there and I'm going to do my race the best that I can. If he beats me, fine. But no, that guy doesn't exist."

—"Crazy John," B-Fuel Harley pilot, Rutland, Iowa, 1991

Street Drags, Beulah, Wyoming, 1995

Sundance Burnout, Sundance, Wyoming 1999

It doesn't take much to get a crowd going, especially when everyone is waiting for something to happen. In the small town of Sundance on Wyoming Wednesday, just rev your engine and you will have a good crowd moving in close and cheering you on to burn rubber. People climb on each other for a peek at the action but if you're right up front, you won't be able to get out. I am always keeping an eye out for an escape route, but should the bike get out of control in its five-foot-wide path in Sundance, there isn't one.

122

Parking Lot Burnout, Beulah, Wyoming, 1999

When that sun drops over the horizon and the temperature cools to near perfection, everyone starts moving with more life.
This magic hour has always been my favorite time to photograph people. It is when they light up and their energy begins to sizzle.
Anything can happen.

Doughnuts, Beulah, Wyoming, 1996

There is something nerve-racking about photographing doughnuts. You never know
when that tire will finally grip the pavement and launch the rider through the group
of people surrounding him. Sometimes they just keep going until the tire bursts.
But my favorite was a guy in Sundance who just went round and round
until his pipes, glowing red, fell off.

"Smoke 'em," Sundance, Wyoming, 1994

That's Why We're Here, Sundance, Wyoming, 2002

A Discovery Channel crew followed Billy Lane as he did everything but pamper this bike, all the way
from Florida to South Dakota. Then I shot this beauty from every angle on a perfectly white background
in the studio. The very next day, we rode off to Wyoming to do the Wednesday loop. By the time we
reached Sundance, there was a good crowd waiting for something to happen and Billy was ready to
light it up. So what if this was one of the best bikes of the year? Rubber was everywhere except on
the back wheel. Billy described it to me: "I go out to have a good time and because I love it.
I don't hold myself back. I just want to enjoy the freedom of being who I am."
With over 50 miles to go back to Sturgis, we put the bike in the back of Steve's truck, and I tossed the
keys to my Road King to Billy. There's no one I'd trust with my bike more than Billy.

**Nick's Ecstasy,
Sundance, Wyoming,
2002**

"I feel like Satan coming out
from the depths of hell, coming
through the smoke."

—Nick, on doing a burnout

Flames, Parked at the Oasis, Sturgis, South Dakota, 1993

In the past, you could always say to your friends, "meet you on Main Street."
It was never a problem when there were a few thousand bikers, even a few tens of thousands.
Now they count bikes in the hundreds of thousands, and they are no longer contained by Sturgis.
Huge lines of bikes can be found from Hulett, Wyoming, to Wall, South Dakota, and beyond.

For years, these flamed choppers seemed to have reserved parking in front of the Oasis right next
to the stop sign. Rat was always there with his flamed bike. If he wasn't sitting out there watching
the crowds, you knew you could find him inside.

Commotion at Gunners, Sturgis, South Dakota, 1990

"In the old days you went on a run and it was a run. You didn't know if some guy in a pickup truck
would pull up alongside and blow you off the road like in the movie, run you off the road, or you'd end
up in jail because you were a biker and you were probably carrying drugs and maybe a gun.
And when you got there you wouldn't know if a club would beat you half to death or if you'd get
arrested by the citizens because you beat up some people in a bar. There was lots of things going on
at that time that made it much more of an adventure. It's still an adventure to ride to Sturgis."

—*From an interview with Keith Ball,*

former editor of Easyriders *magazine, June 1991*

Sturgis Drug, Sturgis, South Dakota, 1986

What memories are flashing through their minds? Could they be thinking about the motorcycle parade
through town in the early rally years? Perhaps they are recalling stories from their childhood
when their families told them about the Northern Cheyenne being escorted down Main Street as they
returned from Pine Ridge to their own reservation in Montana 100 years ago?

Back Patches, Sturgis, South Dakota, 1991

"I'm proud to wear my patch in Sturgis. People recognize it, know we are a national club and have been around for a long time. I've had mine for 25 years and I'll do what it takes to keep it. We're always true to our patch."

—Crud, Sons of Silence, Colorado, 2003

Downtown at Ingalls, Sturgis, South Dakota, 1984

Harass the Police, Sturgis, South Dakota, 1980

All for fun, fun for all. We laughed together and at each other. Have we become more serious?

**John Kay and
Steppenwolf Play
the Hills, Sturgis,
South Dakota, 1987**

Could anything be better than John
Kay and Steppenwolf playing
"Born to Be Wild" in the Black Hills
as a Harley-Davidson revs its
engine on stage, Rusty Dennis
(the woman Cher played in the film
Mask) looking on, and a host
of bikers cheering wildly, singing
along as they hear, "Get your motor
runnin', head out on the highway?"

This is their anthem and for this
one short time each year, this is
their place. This is Sturgis.

Bobber at the Bar & Lounge, Sturgis, South Dakota, 1979

Lit by a powerful flash, this image reminds me of old police photographs. It could have
been taken in 1947 during the Hollister incident and appeared in *Life* magazine. But this is
still the way it was in Sturgis in 1979. I feel too young to have taken it.

WCW at Lynn's, Sturgis, South Dakota, 1999

The Kiss, Deadwood, South Dakota, 1993

As Tammy Wynette sang: "Stand by your man. . . ."

There is nothing like taking a ride with your date or, better yet, your love. No other public moments, even dancing, put a man and woman so close together, let alone on a small seat on what has often been referred to as a "Milwaukee Vibrator." Out with the wind in their faces, exposed to the elements with the hard pavement just a few feet away. And the woman's legs wrapped so tightly around her man for so long. It has changed some. It is acceptable these days for women to ride their own bikes, and the bikes don't vibrate like they used to, but the underlying mystique will always be there.

We're From Texas, Aladdin, Wyoming, 1996

The Marlboro Man, frozen in time, stands guard. The sentry meets his match. Images collide,

then merge in this one-horse town.

Riding Down Main, Sturgis, South Dakota, 1992

"Riding on the back of a bike? Ohhhhhh. What can I say? I feel like I almost had an orgasm.
Just the vibration of the bike. All of that power between my legs. And then, David, who I love,
in front of me, to hold on to. I can't think of anything that feels better than that. It's such a sensual
experience. It releases everything in me."

—From an interview with Joannie, Sturgis, 1992

Stunt Rider at the Strip,
Sturgis, South Dakota, 1997

A warm night at the track. Mouths drop open as the stunt rider makes wheelie

passes in front of the stands. Brought in as an entertainment break, his skill quickly

impresses the crowd of bikers who understand just how tough this is.

They cheer, never seeming to get enough.

Nuclear Burnout, Sturgis, South Dakota, 1988

Being at the track is being in another world. Senses overload and photography is difficult.
Standing close to the bikes, you try to protect yourself as there is much to watch out for. The crack
of the throttle at the start exceeds the limits of what your eardrums can withstand. The rear tire pelts
molten rubber at you that sticks to your skin. Breathing is difficult as you choke on the nitro-methane
fumes. The nitro also causes your eyes to flood with tears to the point you can hardly keep them open.
Add to all of this the 100-degree temperatures, no shade, and lack of drinking water and you begin
to understand how much everyone must love this sport to keep coming back for more.

Flashback, All-Harley Drags, Sturgis, South Dakota, 1987

Explosive sound, nitrous, and tension fill the air. There is electricity at the start. It is dark and it is
the final pass. Everyone is moving quickly to get the machines started, warmed up, and in position.
Cameras flash.

End of an Era, City Park Drags, Sturgis, South Dakota, 1981

City Park was the place to be. There were few options, so Sturgis, with a laissez-faire attitude, turned the park over to bikers, so long as what was done in the park stayed in the park and nobody got hurt. We were all there just to ride and have fun, but by today's standards it got a little out of hand. There was a lot of drinking and drugs. Women would climb up on top of a camping bus and in no time, a huge cheering crowd was there to watch. Late at night, spontaneous drag racing would erupt in the narrow lanes between the tents.

The townspeople said they hated what went on, although enough of them parked on the main road and watched from a distance. Somehow, the police never came into the park, or at least they weren't supposed to. It was like a safe haven. It didn't take much to shut down the park. When campers became upset that the portable toilets weren't being taken care of and torched them, that was it. The next year, the park was closed to camping.

Caught in the Light, Sturgis, South Dakota, 1990

A wild buck out of its element, torn skin, muscles flexed for flight, startled by the light.

Drummer's View, Dancing at the Chip, Sturgis, South Dakota, 1991

Like some sort of ancient ritual, women get on stage to tantalize the already worked-up crowd.
Many have never been naked in front of strangers before, but somehow, at midnight on a concert
stage in the middle of the Black Hills, they choose to perform. This too is part of Sturgis.

On the Horn, City Park, Sturgis, South Dakota, 1979

Blue Night, Sturgis, South Dakota, 1988

It is great to ride through town, weaving the streets, on a warm summer night. You feel like it is all yours, but not in real time or even in the real world. There is an abstract quality, like a swirl of streetlights.

153

Sidelit, Sturgis, South Dakota, 1991

Slinging Ink, Sturgis, South Dakota, 1996

Flash on display, artists at work, machines buzzing. A decision is made that will last a lifetime.

They will be open late into the night. The parlor glows, the sun sets, a bike roars down the alley.

Branscombe Richmond and Eric Runningpath Perform, Downtown Sturgis, South Dakota, 2002

As vice president of Indian Affairs for Indian Motorcycle Corporation, Branscombe Richmond travels all over the country. On occasion, he dons his actor-entertainer cap and gets up on stage to do what he does best: perform. Branscombe says it doesn't matter whether he performs before 30 or 30,000 people, or what their nationality or color is, because as a music lover, he knows that music is an international language and performing feels right.

Downtown Sturgis is Indian country for Branscombe. He believes anyone of native ancestry realizes the Black Hills are a sacred place, so performing here is special, especially with Eric Runningpath, a Navajo and Indian Country ambassador to the U.N. from Window Rock, Arizona, who dances alongside. Have we come full circle in this dance of life?

Masked Biker, Sturgis, South Dakota, 1993

Main Street Sturgis is alive during these hot August nights. Some citizens are still out watching the parade of bikers roll past, but mostly it is bikers watching each other. Some are dressed (or undressed) as if in a performance. Others, like the masked biker, may hide their identity but still expose who they are for all to see.

American Family, Sturgis, South Dakota, 1997

Nighttime near the Night Owl, Sturgis, South Dakota, 1984

"We tried to avoid the police, so we took the kind of roundabout way of getting home. Well, we come across this little town and come to one bar and it was closed and went to the other bar in town. It was on a Sunday, I guess. Had a little fun there, did a few burnouts in front, and the guy opened the bar for us. A nice little goddamned town, you know? We was havin' a good time, and we tried to find this town this year. So me and Billy were drivin' down tryin' to think of the name of this town. I says, 'What the hell's the name of that town Billy?' He says, 'Goddamn, I can't remember the name of that fuckin' goddamned town.' And he says, 'I think it starts with a C.' So we're drivin' around and all of a sudden we come across, here's this sign. What's the name of that town, Billy? Coalworth.

"So we pull into Coalworth and we go in there and we're just havin' a good time and here's the guy, he's a pretty good egg. And they have really good chow in there. And his daughter is just a little flower and you know last year I had the eyes for her a little bit. But she blossomed right up there. I'll tell you what. What do you say, Billy, about a 38D cup now, for a sixteen year old gal? You know my mind was runnin' amuck right then. It kind of turned to Jello. And they started looking at the gold and I says, 'I can get you a good deal on the gold you know.' The gal's lookin' at it so much and she's impressin' me bigtime 'cause I'm a titty man to beat hell. So I just felt real generous, so I take off my goddamn rope chain. I was snapped up a little bit Billy, you know, but I took that off and give it to her. I'll tell you what, the last impression will last forever with that gal. She'll be mine in a couple of years, I guarantee you that. We don't do nothin' under eighteen you know. We're just havin' a good time."

—From an interview with Captain Hook, Rochester, Minnesota, July 1991

**Boondocks, Black Hills,
South Dakota, 1997**

I came across Boondocks late
one night as I was riding through
the hills. Riding around a corner,
the beautiful neon appeared in the
distance in the middle of nowhere.
How could I not have stopped for
a burger and shake?

PHOTOGRAPHER'S NOTES

The style of my photography has evolved over the years and continues to do so to this day. It has always reflected the way I react to the world around me. One thing that hasn't changed is that when I am shooting for myself, or showing my own photography as in the case of this book, images are never cropped or altered. What you see is the full frame, from edge to edge, as canted or cocked as it was in the viewfinder. While it would be easy to move or eliminate elements to improve a photograph, I have chosen to show it as it is or not show it at all.

Country Store, Kentucky, 1976

For those interested in the more technical side of my photography, I can say I used whatever tools seemed best for the given time and situation. Almost all of the images were taken with 35mm cameras, the exception being some medium format black-and-white film that I shot with a $10 plastic-lens camera in 1999. In the 1970s, the cameras were manual focus, manual exposure, fixed lenses like the Nikon FM and F2. I moved to the F3 and F4 in the 1980s, and then to more automatic cameras like Nikon F5s in the 1990s. More recently, I have started to use digital cameras like the Nikon D1 and D1X. Even the automatic cameras were set on manual exposure for the most control, and to this day, regardless of camera, I only use manual flashes.

Mother and Children, Southern Morocco, 1978

As for film, there was more diversity. I mostly used Kodak films, going back to when I shot only black and white and always with Kodak Plus-X Pan. I also shot Kodak Tri-X as well as Ilford XP1 and XP2 for black and white. For color, I only shot transparency film, which is what magazines expect. In the earlier years, this meant Kodak Kodachrome 64, but eventually, as they improved, I changed to E-6 films. For the past ten years, I have mostly shot Kodak's E series films, particularly their E-100, but I also shot Fuji E6 films at times and, on rare occasions, Fuji Velvia for its ultra-saturated color.

Southern Watermelon Stand, 1976

Many of the photographs in this book are available as limited-edition prints. For more information, please visit www.lichterphoto.com or e-mail me at Mike@lichterphoto.com.

Credits and Bibliography

Sturgis, The First Fifty Years by Dr. Maz Harris, copyright 1991, Six-Fifty Publications.
Fort Meade & The Black Hills by Robert Lee, copyright 1991, University of Nebraska Press.
Life's Bits and Pieces by Pappy Hoel, copyright 1982, published by Pappy Hoel.
Black Elk Speaks by Nicholas Black Elk, as told through John G. Neihardt, copyright 1932, University of Nebraska Press.

Much information came from numerous websites dedicated to the Sturgis Rally and Races. I would like to thank Robert Lee for checking the introduction for accuracy and to Pearl Hoel, who, in several lengthy conversations, offered first-person accounts of the early rally years.

About the Author

Beggars, Eastern Iran, 1978

Dancer in Drag, India, 1975

Many factors make Michael Lichter's photography distinct, such as his technical mastery, his attention to detail, and his drive for perfection. But page through the images in this book and one factor will stand out above all the rest: his eye. Michael simply sees the world a bit differently than the rest of us. He sees beauty in the way light dances over a scene, beauty that a less sensitive eye might miss. He sees nobility in a face that others might see as threatening or might dismiss entirely. He sees determination where others might see insanity. Perhaps a few other people see the world as Michael does, but no one else captures that vision on film the way he does.

Michael began taking pictures and working in the darkroom at the age of 13, when his father loaned him a WWII-era Pentacon 35mm camera. After graduating from high school, Michael went off to live with a group of photographers at Apeiron Workshops, a "photo farm" in Millerton, New York. He then attended the University of Colorado in Boulder with a major in Fine Arts. Michael supplemented his academic education with extended travels through Asia, Europe, Afghanistan, Iran, Algeria, and the Sudan. Michael is grateful for having had the opportunity to travel through that part of the world in a more peaceful time.

After a short stint playing drums in a bebop jazz band in 1976 and 1977, Michael decided he was a better photographer than drummer and hung up his sticks. It was during this time that he started riding a 1971 Harley-Davidson (which he still owns) and photographing bikers. This work, along with a series on cowboys, made it into many group exhibitions as well as two larger solo exhibitions, one at the Gallery of Photography in Dublin, Ireland (which was boycotted by the League of Decency), and the other in Boulder at the University Memorial Center Gallery. Michael stumbled into commercial photography by selling some of these photographs to magazines.

In 1978 Michael started doing commercial photography in Boulder, Colorado. By 1980, he had worked his passion for motorcycling into his photography career. His work began to appear in *Easyriders* magazine. Soon Michael found himself in the beds of pickup trucks during rainstorms, photographing packs of bikers on the roads around Sturgis, South Dakota, on assignment for the magazine. Capturing Sturgis on film became something of a habit–he's photographed the rally for *Easyriders* every year since 1981.

In 1981, Michael met Catherine, a wonderful Irish woman vacationing in the United States. The following year he married her. They have two children, Kiera, born in 1985, and Sean, born in 1988.

In 1982, Michael opened a studio specializing in photographing motorcycles. After photographing more than 700 feature stories on motorcycles and the biker lifestyle, including more than 60 magazine covers, Michael has returned to exhibiting and selling prints of his work.

Steve Temple, a Cal Poly, San Luis Obispo, graduate has been assisting Michael since 1998. Federica Carrara from Milan, Italy, focuses on digital work, and Catherine Bowe makes certain that the business is headed in the right direction. Over the years, Michael and his team have worked at hundreds of locations around the world, including shoots in Europe, Japan, Canada, and Mexico. Photography involving Harley-Davidson motorcycles comprises about twenty percent of his work. The diverse subject matter comprising the other eighty percent keeps his photography (and his life) exciting.

—Darwin Holmstrom, Editor

Michael on a Flathead, Egypt, 1978

On the Ganges, Varanassi, India, 1975

Village Policeman, Northern Afghanistan, 1975

Weekly Rodeo, South Dakota, 1973

ACKNOWLEDGMENTS

I would like to thank Steve Temple who has worked with me on commercial and motorcycling assignments for five years, including five trips to Sturgis. He gave 110 percent of himself to get this book to press. I would also like to thank Federica Carrara, who worked hard on this project, and Dave Budd and Doug Kamicar who assisted me in Sturgis in the past.

I'm grateful to alpha-biker Peter Fonda, the voice of an entire generation of motorcyclists, for writing the foreword and to Dave Nichols, editor of *Easyriders* magazine for his kind introduction.

Darwin Holmstrom, acquisitions editor at Motorbooks International, supported this project from our first conversation. He had incredible patience and the ability to encourage me to keep going. Art director Becky Pagel had a Zen-like attitude in dealing with me and my requests. I hope I wasn't too hard on her. I also want to thank Doug France for his enthusiasm in pushing the book further.

This book would not be possible without the support of the entire staff at *Easyriders* magazine, particularly editor Dave Nichols and past editors Keith Ball and Frank Kaisler, who gave me great assignments dating back to 1980. Editors Kim Peterson, Scott McCool, and Dean Shawler also supported my efforts. Billy Tinney got me in the door, and without the support of publisher Joe Teresi, very little of this work would exist.

Susan Jacobs helped alleviate my feelings of uncertainty about my writing skills. Photocraft Labs, my professional lab in Boulder, Colorado, came through with superb scanning, processing, and unprecedented turnaround of the scans. Author Robert Lee's book *Fort Meade & the Black Hills* proved invaluable, as did Lee's personal advice. Pearl Hoel was kind enough to send me a copy of Pappy's book *Life's Bits and Pieces*. Our lengthy conversations regarding the history of the rally helped bring this book to life.

My parents, George and Ishka, encouraged me and made it possible for me to pursue photography from an early age, even though they hated the fact that I was in the darkroom printing until 4 a.m. as a kid.

Heartfelt thanks go to the many people who have been the subject of my camera, and particularly to those who are no longer with us. Photography has an amazing ability to keep their memories alive. As life becomes more complicated around us each year, I trust that all the people whose paths I have crossed on this journey find the wonderful freedom and peace that comes with riding on the open road.

INDEX OF PHOTOGRAPHS

Following page:

**Home on the Range,
Sturgis, South Dakota,
1988**

A bike, a tent, and the open plains. You and the elements. Motorcycling teases you with the freedom to be on the road, stop when and where you want, slow down and experience the world first hand.